A P-47 Thunderbolt restored in the colors of the 513th Fighter Squadron, Ninth Air Force flies fast and low over a rail line in Indiana. The sight was a common one over northern France in 1944.

Designed by Dan Patterson. Edited by Meghan M. Mitchell.

Library of Congress Catalog Card Number: 98-74028

ISBN 1-57427-053-2

Printed in Hong Kong

Published by Howell Press, Inc.
1713-2D Allied Lane
Charlottesville, VA 22903
(804) 977-4006
http://www.howellpress.com

10 9 8 7 6 5 4 3 2 1

HOWELL PRESS

Previous page: Selected fighter pilot gear. At top left is a Twelfth Air Force silk scarf; to its right sits a propeller manual from Curtiss Electric. At center right, inside the webbing from an American, seat-style parachute, is a Royal Air Force life jacket with survival items in the right pocket. At bottom right a field maintenance manual for the P-47 lies open. The green B-10 flight jacket at left replaced the famous leather A-2 late in the war. On top of it are the pilot's flight helmet, goggles, and oxygen mask.

Preface

Each of these "Living History" books is an attempt to look through a window on the past, an attempt to recreate what once was. That's basic to any study of history, and it's our good fortune to live at a time when turning back the clock isn't quite the struggle it might be. At the time of the American Civil War, for example, photography was in its infancy; films were very slow, and optics were only beginning to be understood. The historians who write about that war have the written record, but the advantages of audio recordings and film accrue only to those of us concerned with later times. We have another advantage over the Civil War historian: the veterans of World War II are still with us, though their numbers are dwindling. We have a golden if fleeting opportunity to try to know what they know.

The window that lets us look back is multilayered. It's the opportunity to talk with those who were there. It's the chance to see the few examples of their tools, the machines of war that remain. To watch and listen to historic moments recorded and preserved on film and in magazines and books. It falls to us, with the help of modern technology and the perspective that only time can give, to translate that information into a meaningful view.

The restored fighters and bombers that are my subjects are single examples of the vast fleets of warplanes that men flew and fought in over the battlefields of Europe. These sorts of events will not happen again, thank God; the technology that grew from the conflict that was World War II made massed formations filled with young men unnecessary. Where once a formation of hundreds of bombers escorted by further hundreds of fighters was required to destroy a target, a score of cruise missiles, controlled by computer and directed by satellite, now does the job.

I am an unabashed fan of just about anything that flies. I admit it, and I can't help it. I grew up in the city of the Wright brothers, and Orville died just a few years before I came along. I found it fascinating to hear people say, "Yeah, I used to have lunch at the Van Cleve, and Orville always ate lunch at his table, over there." The Van Cleve Hotel has since been made into a parking lot, but I remember the thrill of being in a room where he had once been. I get the same thrill when I go to Thomas Jefferson's Monticello or stand in the Battle of Britain control room, where Douglas Bader was once in charge. These are also windows on the past.

Only the veterans of World War II can truly know what it took to get up every day and go to war in these machines. Only they can remember what it was like to hear hundreds of these engines. But it could be said that I—and you, in the book in your hands—have the next best thing. My favorite moment as I work on these projects is when the engine starts, when Mike (dressed in the appropriate leather jacket, flight helmet, and yellow life vest) climbs into the cockpit and brings the big fighter slowly to life. The whine of the oil pump and the servos that open the cowl flaps precedes the slow turning of the huge four-bladed propeller. After several revolutions, he engages the starter, and the prop jerks and the exhaust stacks belch blue smoke. The prop turns and stops and turns and stops—and then the big radial engine starts, the black propeller spinning into a blur, its painted tips etching a yellow circle. Excess oil pours from the stacks as the engine settles into a pleasant roar.

I love my job.

Dan Patterson
January 12, 1999

THUNDERBOLT
Republic P-47

Photographs by Dan Patterson
Text by Paul Perkins

Howell Press

The Seversky P-35, forerunner of the Thunderbolt.   USAFM

In the mid-1930s, Col. Henry H. Arnold of the United States Army Air Corps (USAAC) and some of his contemporaries believed that liquid-cooled in-line engines would power the bombers and fighters of the future. These same engines would also power lightweight fighter interceptors charged with defending the United States against enemy bombers.

Given the range of existing and foreseeable bomber designs, it is not clear where such a bomber threat would originate. Nevertheless, in 1939, Arnold's vision took the form of Circular Proposal CP39-770. On August 1 of that year, Alexander Kartveli, chief designer for the Seversky Aircraft Corporation, proposed a lightweight, high-altitude interceptor to the USAAC under the company designation of AP-10. The AP-10 would be powered by the 1,150-horsepower Allison V-1710-39 liquid-cooled in-line engine.

The Allison in-line engine had a small frontal area that allowed for a streamlined airframe design. Glycol coolant, more efficient than water at carrying off engine heat, also made possible smaller radiators and less drag. Gross weight would be 4,900 pounds; estimated

maximum speed, 415 MPH. Armament was to be a pair of .50-caliber machine guns mounted in the engine housing. As planned, the AP-10 would resemble such contemporary European fighters as the Messerschmitt Bf 109, the Supermarine Spitfire, and the very beautiful French Dewoitine D.520.

The USAAC looked over the proposal and was favorably impressed. The corps believed, however, that additional armament would be required, even if it adversely affected performance. Kartveli increased his AP-10's size and added four wing-mounted .30-caliber machine guns. Gross weight rose to 6,570 pounds. In November 1939, the USAAC ordered one prototype of this altered design under the designation XP-47. On January 17, 1940, the USAAC ordered a stripped, unarmed version that was denoted XP-47A.

In the meantime, reports coming in from Europe were changing everyone's ideas about air combat. More firepower, more armament, more protective armor, and self-sealing fuel tanks would likely be required in future battles. The XP-47 didn't have sufficient engine power to accommodate the additional weight of such

features, and the USAAC ultimately concluded that it was unlikely to be a future combat standout.

By that time, using the Allison in-line engine had forced a radical change in design philosophy for Kartveli. He had developed a preference for aircraft with air-cooled radial engines, which were simpler to design and could absorb a greater amount of damage, and had begun tinkering with spin-offs of his Seversky P-35 while working with the in-line engine. The P-35, along with the Curtiss P-36, constituted the backbone of USAAC's pursuit aircraft branch during the late 1930s. Armed only with two .30-caliber machine guns, the P-35 was a low-wing, radial-engine monoplane with retractable landing gear.

The P-35 evolved into the P-43 Lancer, which was essentially a turbocharged P-35. The P-43 had in turn evolved into the P-44 Rocket. Kartveli had never given up on the concept of a radial-engine fighter, and the necessities of war now gave him his hand.

He crafted a new high-altitude interceptor, dubbed the P-47, around the newly available Pratt & Whitney R-2800 Twin Wasp, an

Republic P-47 prototype.

USAFM

eighteen-cylinder, air-cooled radial engine that was among the most powerful of its time. He designed the fuselage around the combined turbosupercharger assembly and engine. To ensure a streamlined fuselage with a small cross section, the turbosupercharger was positioned near the rear of the fuselage, where it was fed by air ducts located beneath the engine. Other ductwork carried exhaust gases aft to the turbine. These were vented under the tail, just forward of the tail wheel. Air compressed by the exhaust-driven turbosupercharger was returned forward to the engine through still more ductwork. More than thirty percent of a P-47's fuselage interior was taken up by the turbosupercharger and related assemblies! Turbosupercharging enabled the R-2800 to produce ample power from sea level to more than 30,000 feet.

Taking advantage of the R-2800's tremendous might required a four-bladed propeller twelve feet in diameter. The Curtiss Electric variable pitch propeller was the first four-bladed unit to be mounted on a U.S. military aircraft.

The propeller, too, affected the aircraft's design. To ensure that its blades cleared the ground during takeoff and landing, the P-47 was outfitted with a long undercarriage. A landing gear that retracted in the conventional way, meanwhile, would have required attachment too far outboard on the wings to allow for the proposed eight wing guns and their ammunition. The solution was a landing gear that telescoped when retracted, making it nine inches shorter when withdrawn than when extended.

All of the Thunderbolt's fuel, totaling 305 gallons, was carried in two large fuselage tanks. Armament, eight .50-caliber machine guns in the wings, reflected the Royal Air Force's emphasis on eight-gun fighters. The total weight of this single-seat fighter was to be an unprecedented 11,500 pounds, making it one of the heaviest armed fighters considered by the USAAC up to that time. The P-47 had gone from aerial ballerina to heavyweight boxer.

Republic Aircraft Corporation, as Seversky had been renamed in late 1939, submitted this concept to the USAAC on June 12, 1940. The corps was evidently impressed with Kartveli's work; on September 6 of that same year, it ordered a prototype under the designation XP-47B.

Assigning the same pursuit number designation to a completely new design was unusual. All work on the diminutive XP-47 and XP-47A was canceled. The serial number of the aborted XP-47 was transferred to the XP-47B.

Just one week after its initial order, on September 13, 1940, the USAAC requisitioned 773 production examples of the Thunderbolt, simultaneously canceling a 1939 contract for 80 P-44 Rockets. The canceled contract was replaced by an order for a similar quantity of P-43 Lancers meant to keep the Farmingdale, New York, production lines occupied pending the introduction of the P-47.

Test pilot Lowry L. Brabham took the XP-47B aloft for the first time on May 6, 1941, a mere eight months after USAAC had placed its initial order. On this first flight, Brabham was forced to make an unplanned emergency landing when the cockpit filled with smoke from oil cooking off the exhaust trunking.

In 1941, the XP-47B was the largest single-engine fighter ever built. At empty and loaded gross weights of 9,189 pounds and 12,086 pounds, respectively, it was almost twice as heavy as most of its contemporaries and dwarfed all previous fighters. The turbosupercharging enabled the engine to deliver 1,960 horsepower at 25,800 feet and gave the XP-47B a maximum speed of 412 MPH, 12 MPH faster than Kartveli had projected. An altitude of 15,000 feet could be attained in five minutes. The prototype was destroyed in an accident on August 8, 1942.

The first production P-47B was delivered on December 21, 1941. Five more were delivered in March 1942, only ten months after the XP-47B had first flown. Numerous problems arose as the test program advanced, delaying further P-47B acceptances until May. At altitudes above 30,000 feet, ailerons snatched and froze, the cockpit canopy could not be opened, and control forces became excessive. Republic engineers solved the problem of the freezing ailerons by covering the control surfaces of subsequent P-47Bs with metal. The ailerons were altered in shape and fitted with blunt noses, which alleviated the problem of excessive control forces. Balanced trim tabs were adopted to reduce rudder pedal loads. A rearward sliding hood replaced the original hinged canopy, which solved the stuck cockpit canopy problem but meant that the dorsal radio antenna had to be redesigned and moved aft.

Production P-47Bs were fitted with 2,000-horsepower R-2800-21 engines, which made greater amounts of internal equipment possible without any sacrifice in performance. While maximum loaded weight increased to 13,360 pounds, maximum speed at 27,000 feet burgeoned to 429 MPH. The Thunderbolt's initial climb rate was 2,560 feet per minute; an altitude of 15,000 feet could be attained in 6.7 minutes. The aircraft's service ceiling was 42,000 feet. Range without extra ordnance at maximum cruising power was 550 miles at 335 MPH at 10,000 feet.

The United States officially entered the Second World War after the Japanese attack on Pearl Harbor, on December 7, 1941. To bolster the air defenses around New York City and other industrial targets in the Northeast, various

squadrons were moved to New England coastal areas. The Fifty-sixth Fighter Group (FG), created scarcely a year previously and equipped mostly with Bell P-39 Airacobras, had its three squadrons at Bridgeport, Connecticut; Bendix, New Jersey; and Farmingdale, in close quarters with the Republic plant. All three squadrons of the Eightieth, another new fighter group, went to Farmingdale. Both the Fifty-sixth and the Eightieth were equipped with P-47Bs for stateside testing and operational training. The Fifty-sixth, which was issued Thunderbolts in mid-1942, found the task of working up its new

P-47Ds on the way to war.   USAFM

fighters especially difficult; thirteen pilots and forty-one aircraft were lost in accidents. Republic engineers were frequently called upon to help iron out problems.

The last of the P-47Bs was delivered in September 1942. One final example of the series was converted during manufacture into the XP-47E, which featured a pressurized cockpit and the old-style hinged canopy. This version never made it into production. Another P-47B airframe became an XP-47F; this prototype tested a new, larger wing with a laminar flow airfoil. It flew for the first time on September 17, 1942. No production was undertaken.

The first P-47Cs came off the production lines at Farmingdale in late September 1942. They differed from the B model in many respects and are generally regarded as the first truly combat worthy Thunderbolts. The fuselage held a new engine mounting and was extended forward of the fire wall by eight inches. The joint between the aft fuselage and the tail section was strengthened, and from the beginning the control surfaces of each were metal covered. The P-47B's forward-slanted radio antenna mast was replaced by a shorter, upright mast, and the rudder and elevator balance systems were completely revamped. An improved and higher capacity oxygen system completed the renovation.

Republic sent two P-47Cs to the Army Air Force (AAF) School of Applied Tactics at Orlando, Florida. In comparative tests and mock air combat exercises opposite a Lockheed P-38F, Bell P-39D-1, Curtiss P-40F, and North American P-51A, the P-47C's top speeds, particularly at high altitude, surprised everyone. Getting to high altitude, however, was a problem. The P-47Cs couldn't climb any faster than 3,000 feet per minute. An ascent to 20,000 feet took fourteen minutes.

Mock combat revealed a Thunderbolt advantage in rate of roll, dive acceleration, and level flight acceleration. The P-47's turning radius, however, was the largest of the group and a real liability. On the other hand, a P-47 could roll into a reverse turn and break off combat at will—a great advantage. The key to success in the P-47, as in any other fighter, lay in determining what it did best and never engaging an opponent in any maneuver at which he excelled.

Normal combat range—only 550 miles from 305 gallons—was another of the Thunderbolt's limitations. This lack of endurance was addressed in later production blocks of P-47Cs by the provision of under-fuselage shackles that enabled one 200-gallon drop tank to be carried. This extended the range to 1,250 miles at an altitude of 10,000 feet and a cruising speed of 231 MPH. Later P-47Cs had engines that were capable of water injection. This gave a brief war emergency power of 2,300 horsepower. Just over six hundred P-47Cs were delivered by February 1943, when the P-47D replaced it on the production line.

Thunderbolts began to arrive in Britain in November 1942. Pilots of the Fourth FG, used to flying the graceful Supermarine Spitfires, were aghast at the immensity of the P-47s that replaced them. Another group, the Seventy-eighth, had been flying P-38 Lightnings until its aircraft were commandeered for Operation Torch.

On April 8, 1943, in a fighter sweep "rodeo" over Dieppe, France, the Fourth FG, Eighth Air Force became the first unit to fly an operation with Thunderbolts. The P-47C's first encounter with German fighters came on April 15, when the 335th Squadron shot down three German fighters and suffered an identical loss. This kill/loss ratio, of course, would improve over time.

Not long after this debut, the fighter's mission began to evolve. Early in WWII, most U.S. strategists maintained that unescorted mass formations of fast, heavily armed bombers could penetrate an enemy's airspace. Flying high would foil antiaircraft batteries; sufficient speed would enable the bombers to outrun any fighter that the formation's incredible collective firepower could not discourage.

Unfortunately for the Eighth Air Force, unescorted raids on such German targets as Schweinfurt and Regensburg revealed that even box formations with murderously intense interlocking fields of defensive fire failed to deter the Luftwaffe. As the U.S. ratcheted up its daylight bombing campaign, the Luftwaffe steadily improved its tactics and ability to kill unescorted bombers. The idea of unescorted bombers became less and less palatable as losses escalated, and Thunderbolts were quickly pressed into service. Their first escort mission was on May 4, 1943.

At high altitude, the performance of the P-47C was far superior to that of anything the Luftwaffe could put up against it. Besides its superior roll rate, the P-47C could out-dive just about anything in the sky, giving its pilots a handy avenue of escape should one become necessary. Pilots were cautioned, however, against carrying the battle below 20,000 feet. At low and medium altitudes the P-47C could not match the maneuverability and climb rates of its opponents.

Ultimately, the Luftwaffe's most effective means of dealing with Thunderbolts involved exploiting the P-47's still-inadequate range. German pilots waited until the big Republic fighters were forced home by low fuel to move

sory section had been redesigned. Armor protection for the pilot was more extensive. Even so, early P-47Ds can be distinguished from Cs only by their serial numbers.

Demand for the Thunderbolt was so great that Republic built a new factory, at Evansville, Indiana, to augment production of the P-47D. The USAAF also contracted Curtiss-Wright to build D models under license at its plant in Buffalo, New York. Curtiss-Wright Thunderbolts were designated P-47Gs and can be distinguished from Republic Thunderbolts only by their serial numbers.

A P-47 Thunderbolt carrying pressed paper drop tanks under each wing. USAFM

in on bombers; they also used feinting attacks to prompt Thunderbolts to jettison their drop tanks prematurely. Much subsequent development and modification of the P-47 was directed at trying to shoehorn a high-altitude point interceptor into the role of a long-range, strategic escort fighter.

The P-47D was the first version of the Thunderbolt to undergo truly large scale production. In its initial form, the P-47D differed very little from the P-47C. Improvements had been made to the turbosupercharger exhaust system, which on the D model incorporated an adjustable duct, and vents for the engine acces-

Later blocks of P-47Ds featured shackles for a belly tank or a 500-pound bomb, provision for underwing drop tanks, and a more powerful R-2800 63 engine. These Thunderbolts were outfitted with stronger wing and underwing pylons, which enabled them to carry two 1,000-pound bombs, three 500-pound bombs (one on each wing and one on the fuselage centerline), or a combination of bombs and drop tanks.

It's always been true that the enemy fighter that gets you is the one you do not see, and the Thunderbolt's subpar rearward visibility also got a boost. A few P-47s were fitted with the

An escorting P-47 is silhouetted by contrails created by 390th Bomber Group B-17s.

During the two months leading up to June 6, 1944, these Allied air forces carried out interdiction attacks against rail centers. A bridge-busting campaign, designed to isolate the battle-field by cutting Seine River bridges below Paris and Loire River bridges below Orleans, began on D-Day minus 46. Fighter-bombers such as Thunderbolts proved more efficient than medium or heavy bombers at this endeavor; their agility made possible pinpoint attacks that larger bombers, committed to horizontal runs, could not match. Thunderbolts had the speed, fire-power, and maneuverability to evade or even dominate what remained of the Luftwaffe.

By D-Day minus 21, Allied air forces were hammering German airfields within a 130-mile radius of the battle area. These operations continued until June 6.

"Then shall the right aiming thunderbolts go abroad; and from the clouds, as from a well drawn bow, shall they fly to the mark."
—*Wisdom of Solomon*, Book 6, Verse 21

Late Spring 1944 — 2245 hours:

While you are sleeping, the group S-2 intelligence duty officer (IO) glances at the yellow paper fresh from the Teletype, signs the message, and retires. This is a warning order—an official tip that higher headquarters is considering a mission to Dreux, France. It's early yet; the plan may change multiple times before the fighters actually take off.

0100 HRS: The Teletype operator rousts the IO and hands him another message—the field order. The show is on. The IO rouses the duty operations officer. The two begin the process of making plans for the group's mission. The IO also notifies and provides preliminary information to the group leader, the pilots, the engineering section, the weather officer, and all of the other people involved in mission preparation.

The IO estimates the time of takeoff (0830 HRS) and works backward from that point to establish the briefing time (about one hour

Spitfire's Malcolm Hood, which gave a less obstructed view. In July 1943, engineers modified an early block P-47D-5 by cutting down the fuselage aft of the cockpit and fitting it with the bubble canopy from a British Hawker Typhoon. This worked very well and was immediately introduced on all P-47 production lines. A radical change in appearance resulted, but the USAAF elected merely to assign new block numbers to the P-47D production lines.

Other sizable alterations accompanied the canopy change. To address the problem of anemic climb rate, Curtiss Electric units were replaced with "paddle bladed" Hamilton Standard propellers. These propellers, which had wider blades and an extra foot of diameter, yielded a 400-feet-per-minute improvement in the climb rate. The internal fuel capacity of later P-47Ds, 370 gallons, was also an improvement.

Toward the end of 1943, Eighth Air Force Thunderbolts were given permission to return from escort missions over the Continent "on the deck." Thunderbolts could seek ground targets on their way back to England and were well suited to this new task, though they would never be a long-range strategic fighter in the European Theater of Operations (ETO). The P-51 Mustang, with its much longer legs, would assume this role in 1944 and beyond. In a paradox of war, the high-altitude interceptor became the U.S.'s premier aerial ground pounder in the ETO.

As Operation Overlord, the invasion of western Europe, drew nearer, tactical air power assumed increasing importance. In early 1944, two tactical air forces existed to support the ground forces in the invasion: the AAF's Ninth Air Command, or Ninth Tactical Air Command (TAC), and the Royal Air Force's Second Tactical Air Force.

"I was happy to have been flying '47s (at high altitude) as opposed to the '38s a little later. They were freezing to death up there around 30,000 while we were nice and comfortable. That big radial engine up in front kept us reasonably warm."
— Gordon S. Burlingame, Eighth Air Force, 353rd Fighter Group, 352nd Squadron

Maintenance personnel tend to a P-47 between missions. ^{USAFM}

before engine start, at 0820 HRS), mess hours, rising time for the ground squadrons (0430 HRS or 0500 HRS), and rising time for pilots (0600 HRS).

The intelligence officers join forces to summarize the mission for presentation at the briefing. They describe the target, radio control, emergency facilities, expected enemy reaction, flak defenses, and position of ground troops. They try to present a complete picture to the group leader.

As the S-2 officers finish the briefing boards, the squadron commanding officers (COs) are stirring from the orderly rooms and waking up the mechanics, armorers, radiomen, and others. The engineering and armament sections turn out.

Before eating breakfast, two men for each ship, a mechanic and an armorer, hitch a ride on a truck or grab a bike to ride out to the waiting Thunderbolts. The remaining mechanics and armorers head to the mess for a quick meal; they'll relieve the others shortly.

Not many of the communications men are up, though a few are present to handle any unexpected problems. The radio section worked late last night, examining and testing transmitters and receivers after yesterday's mission, so most of that group is still sleeping.

Out on the line, your crew chief climbs into the cockpit as part of his pre-flight of the P-47 you will fly. Three or four mechanics shoulder one of the four broad Hamilton Standard propeller blades. Together, they manually cycle the big R-2800 to clear out any oil that has accumulated in its lower cylinders since the last flight. The crew chief starts the engine and runs it up for a check. When the propeller stops, the armorer opens the gun compartment on each wing and makes a quick visual exam of the .50-caliber machine guns, ammunition feed chutes, and cartridges. He reaches in and shakes each weapon to ensure that it is securely mounted and will not jar loose while firing. Next, he charges the weapon, closes the compartment, and examines the gunsight. He confirms that the two 500-pound bombs are secure on the shackles and that the bomb fuses and wires are in order.

As the crew chief and armorer finish up, the men who have eaten breakfast arrive. The assistant crew chief now prepares for the compressed oxygen suppliers and the fuel men, who are already servicing nearby planes. Fuel tanks are topped off and oxygen bottles filled. A mechanic cleans off the canopy with a chamois—removing smudges that might have hidden an attacking Luftwaffe fighter.

One mechanic stands waiting by your fighter-bomber. The rest wander off to their shacks to play cards or sleep.

The intelligence officers of Squadrons S-2 and S-3 continue to gather important information, such as flak reports, to post on the briefing board. Operations clerks make last-minute contact with the ground echelon to determine which planes will be available for the mission, who will fly each, and which aircraft have been put back in commission by the night-shift mechanics. Since missions are flown by day, maintenance and repair work can be done only at night. While you and the other pilots sleep, the airfield is alive with activity.

The engineering department reports that forty-eight Thunderbolts from your squadron are ready to go. The men of S-3 pass this information along to the briefer, then relax until it's time to take the pilots out to their fighter-bombers.

Squadron S-2 prepares course cards and maps for you. Accuracy is essential, and navigation is largely visual. A wrong compass bearing on a course card or an error depicting checkpoints on a map could mean chaos in the air.

0600 HRS: Your last few minutes of sleep are disturbed by the sound of heavy bombers thundering overhead toward their formation assembly points. Before you leave the tent, you empty your pockets of any personal identifica-

"First thing we did was synchronize our watches. The start engine time. Just when it started to get light. We'd all start engines at the same time so we'd all consume about the same amount of fuel."
— Charles W. Cassidy, Ninth Air Force, 358th Fighter Group, 367th Squadron

tion: wallet, notebook, latest letter from home. You slide into long johns and heavy socks, then put on olive drab poplin trousers, a shirt with Ninth Air Force insignia, and a scarf. A light cotton flying suit fits over all of this. You double-check your "escape kit"—reichsmarks and francs, waterproof maps printed on linen cloth, concentrated food rations, a couple of candy bars, an extra clip of ammunition for your Colt .45. You stuff all of this in your knee pockets, then sling on the shoulder holster with the heavy Colt. Last, you put on your "leather"—your A-2 flight jacket.

Before trudging through the thinning mist to breakfast, you reflect briefly upon your "will." Who should get your whiskey and candy ration?

0720 HRS: After a meal of powdered eggs, you and your squadron mates straggle into the briefing room. The curtain is pulled back. A wall-size map marked with red tape shows your course and target for the day. The bomb-laden P-47s will attack and destroy the railyard and the bridge on the west side of Dreux. The intelligence officers have also prepared maps showing your course and possible alternate strafing targets should the primary be obscured. You note the targets and wonder how far you might have to walk to Spain should you be unlucky.

You note the mission timetable, displayed on a large board and detailing the time of engine start, when to set course, and when your Mustang top cover will pick you up.

The station weather officer steps to the front. All night, observers and forecasters have made regular readings of temperature, wind velocity, and barometric pressure. Combining this with data from other stations, the weather officer tells you what to expect in the way of clouds and winds at various altitudes along your route. Today's forecast calls for three-quarters scattered coverage from about 12,000 feet down to 8,000 feet . . . Just enough to allow dive-bombing.

After the weatherman finishes, the mission leader takes over. Today the mission leader is

your squadron CO. He is burdened with the weight of command; your group's successful execution of this mission is his responsibility. He points out the flak areas and enemy airfields you may have overlooked.

At the end of the briefing you are issued your mission cards and maps. Before leaving, everyone synchronizes his "hack" watch with that of the group leader.

You head over to the personal equipment locker, where a sergeant signs over your parachute, your collapsible dinghy, and the yellow-orange Mae West life preserver. Traversing the

English Channel takes only a few minutes, but it's a cold swim if you have to ditch or bail out. All of this equipment has been inspected by the base's personal equipment section and by squadron parachute riggers prior to pickup.

You toss your equipment in the back of an ammunition carrier and ride out to your plane. There is a menacing, dedicated beauty about an armed Thunderbolt; slung underneath your craft are a pair of 500-pound bombs (one on each wing) and a 200-gallon centerline drop tank. Your P-47D is named *Jean* after your

girlfriend back in Montana. She only vaguely resembles the voluptuous blonde that graces the left side of the engine cowling.

A mechanic helps you unload your gear and accompanies you on a brief walk around the plane. He tells you what repairs have been made and what might still be a problem. You check the tires and landing gear strut clearances, uncover the pitot tube, and check the caps on the fuselage tanks and drop tank.

You can't get dressed for this party without help. The mechanic helps you with the Mae West and parachute. The dinghy sits on the

A crew chief talks with his pilot before takeoff.

seat.

The mechanic climbs up on the wing and gives you a hand. You hoist yourself along two footholds in the left fuselage, aft of the wing's trailing edge, then scramble along the walkway. You throw one leg in and swing over and down into the seat. The crew chief hovers over you as you plug in your oxygen hose, microphone, and headset. He says a few final words: the usual admonition to bring the bird back in one piece.

He then scrambles out near the left wingtip and lies down, grasping the pitot tube.

With the canopy slid back, you commence your pre-start ritual. Ignition and master batteries are off. Flaps are up. The flap equalizer is set to CLOSED; the generator switch, ON.

Under two minutes to start.

You lean toward the instrument panel and flip the master battery switch up, to ON. Your fingers march methodically across the main switch box, below the throttle quadrant. Intercooler shutters set to NEUTRAL; oil cooler shutters likewise. Propeller switch, ON. Pitch selector, AUTOMATIC. Rotate the fuel booster pump rheostat full counterclockwise, to START

A lineup of Seventy-Eighth Fighter Group Thunderbolts.

USAFM

& ALTITUDE.

Check the fuel selector valve to your left; it should be set to MAIN.

Watch the fuel pressure gauge pump, on the instrument panel's lower right, tick upwards.

Your left hand pulls the supercharger lever full aft, to OFF. Your eyes flit back to the main switch box, to check that the gun switch is set to OFF.

Fewer than sixty seconds to start.

Another mechanic positions himself off to the side, fire extinguisher in hand.

Thirty seconds. You crack the throttle open 1½ inches, set the mixture control to IDLE CUT-OFF, and use the propeller control knob to specify a maximum of 2,700 rpm.

0820 HRS: From the control tower, a flare hisses skyward. The aircraft of two squadrons commence engine start.

Your right hand pumps the engine primer four times. Your left hand flips the ignition switch on the instrument panel to BOTH. Somewhere up front, the beast begins to stir.

You hit the starter. Four Hamilton Standard propeller blades swing past.

With a hesitant bark and rumble a great blue cloud erupts from the exhaust stacks. The engine fires straight up, joining the throaty rumble of nearly fifty Pratt & Whitney radial engines filling the air.

Immediately, you move the mixture control to AUTO-RICH and throttle back to 900 rpm. Your eyes shoot over to the instrument panel's right side, watching the oil pressure climb toward 150 pounds before drifting downward as the oil temperature rises toward 40°C.

You pull the cowl flap handle, just below the primer pump handle, aft to open the cowl flaps; you don't want to fry your ignition wiring harness.

Once you've specified manual control of the propeller, you run through the magneto check. With the throttle open to 2,000 rpm, run up the engine to thirty inches of manifold pressure for one minute. Neither magneto drop exceeds 50 rpm. You cycle your propeller while watching the engine rpm and cast a glance at the ammeter to confirm that the generator is charging.

You verify that the flap lever on your left is full forward and, reaching down with your right hand, open the flap equalizer valve until the rod on the equalizer cylinder slides out about one-half inch. You close the valve and focus your attention just forward of it, on the tail wheel lock handle. You pull it aft to unlock the tail wheel; now it's connected to the rudder.

A P-47 taxies like a Cadillac, but you're without any direct forward vision. Out on the left wing, your crew chief helps you negotiate the narrow taxiway to the run-up area. The fighter-bombers line up abreast next to the runway.

Your crew chief scoots back across the wing and drops to the ground.

You set the trim tabs for takeoff and adjust the mixture control to AUTO-RICH, the propeller control to full forward. Set the propeller switches to ON and AUTOMATIC. Confirm that the fuel selector valve is set to MAIN, and set the flaps at half position. Your left hand pushes the turbine supercharger control knob full forward.

Thirty-six P-47s have taken off. It's your turn. You release the brakes and trundle into position on the runway. Set the brakes. Close and lock the canopy. Reach down and lock the tail wheel.

The P-47 that preceded you is off and climbing. A man standing halfway down the humped turf runway waves a flag. An airman standing off your wing waves his flag in turn.

It's time to go.

You release the brakes, and nearly ten tons of fighter-bomber begin to roll. You advance the throttle until you hit fifty inches of manifold. Add rudder to offset the torque of the engine and propeller, to keep your Thunderbolt accelerating in a straight line.

Nearly 4,000 feet down the runway you and your wingman are aloft. You move the safety latch aside and raise the landing gear. Hydraulic pressure steadily returns to 1,000 PSI. You ease up the flaps, trim the nose down slightly, and gradually reduce the rudder trim.

You check your radios while you are still at low altitude. There is no point in announcing the mission to the Germans, who will know soon enough.

By the time your CO has made two circuits of the airfield, one squadron is up. Two more turns around the field, and both squadrons are aloft. The fighters form up and begin the climb, in groups of four, toward the target area.

As the collective thunder of the formation dies away, the members of your ground crew pick up any scattered tools and equipment, then retire to their shacks for a well-deserved sleep. If sleep does not come, they'll likely play cards or talk.

0845 HRS: The formation passes over the coastal town of Hastings. The English Channel stretches ahead. Beyond it lies occupied France.

0903 HRS: You cross the French coast just west of Dieppe. Already, your top cover lurks overhead. The squadron of P-51 Mustangs is charged with discouraging any attempt by the Luftwaffe to break up your mission.

The cloud cover becomes less broken as you pass Rouen; there's only a smattering of antiaircraft fire.

0918 HRS: Descending through the clouds, you uncage your instruments and concentrate on them until you break clear at 8,500 feet, about ten miles north-northwest of Dreux. Everyone jettisons his drop tank.

0930 HRS: After some visual reconnoitering your group arrives in the vicinity of the target. As the ships slide out of formation and into orbit around Dreux, Germans manning antiaircraft emplacements load and lock. A supply train threads its way through the railyard. The first P-47 rolls into its bombing run.

The first salvo of 500-pound bombs disintegrates rolling stock two tracks over. Debris and smoke erupt into the air and rain down on the station and train, now accelerating toward the west end of the yard.

Another salvo reduces the signal tower to a pile of scrap metal lying across the rails. The train's momentum carries the engine into the wreckage of the tower, where it derails. Relentless, the P-47s position and roll in, one by one, to attack. Others orbit out of antiaircraft range, waiting their turn to pummel the railyard and drop the bridge span on the west side of town.

You're up. You recheck the gun-arming switch to your left. Just behind it is the gun-safety switch; you flip it down, to GUN & CAMERA. A gunsight reticle appears on the windscreen. You arm the bombs.

Zeroing in on a pair of locomotives, you throttle back and wing over into a dive. The airspeed indicator winds up quickly, and you settle in at around 350 MPH. The altimeter winds down. A steam engine on a siding comes under the gunsight pipper.

No rousing patriotic marches play through your headphones; more importantly, no flashing indicators tell you when to drop. There is only your Thunderbolt, your practiced eye, and the target.

Streaks of brightness tear past you: flak. When you begin to hear the flak as well as see it, you'll know it's too close.

As you pass through 3,000 feet above ground level, you raise the nose slightly to give proper lead for the bomb trajectory. Bombs away!

No sooner have they dropped than you

A German supply train receives pre-invasion attention from a P-47.   USAFM

"If we came across a train — the was the most fun of all — we'd star shooting at that boiler, and all of sudden, POOOF! Thick whi smoke would fly up."
— Charles W. Cassidy, Ninth Air Force, 358th Fighter Group, 367th Squadron

begin to pull out and open the throttle. Now 1,000 pounds lighter, your P-47 seems to leap skyward.

In the midst of your zoom climb, a noise like rocks raining on a tin roof pushes in through your headphones. Unflappable, you continue to climb and level off at about 8,000 feet, at last pausing to realize that your bombs landed squarely on target.

Your squadron mates watched you and your wingman settle into a stable dive and drop your bombs. But neither they—nor you—could see the single forty-millimeter cannon shell that lacerated the bottom of your wingman's plane, piercing the main fuselage tank and the floor of the cockpit. In an instant, everything from the lap harness up disappeared—and the freckle-faced kid from Oklahoma was gone. His flaming Thunderbolt roared over the railroad station and across the Rue de Bois before slamming into a building.

Your first inkling that something has gone wrong comes only now, minutes later, when you notice that your wingman does not appear off your right side. As it turns out, his plight isn't the extent of the trouble.

The scattered cloud cover has allowed a pair of FW 190s to slip past the escorting Mustangs. The few Thunderbolts still armed immediately jettison their bombs, throttle up, and ready to meet the new threat. Someone is yelling your name over the radio; one of the FW 190s is closing from behind.

The caller would come to your assistance, but cannon shells off his right wingtip alert him to his own problems. You open throttle and roll right, taking a couple of hits before the German fighter blows on by, headed out of an airspace that's teeming with U.S. fighters.

Reefing about, you try to pick him out, but he's already a fast-receding speck. His leader, caught in the eight .50-calibers of another P-47, is less fortunate; his FW 190 plunges earthward, afire. The skirmish is over as quickly as it began.

1001 HRS: Four flights have picked up the rail line running west-northwest and are

A P-47 gun camera captured the last moments of an FW 190.

following it on the deck, looking for more targets. East of Argentan, you run the tracks as they swing around a ridge. The Normandy countryside opens out in front of you. A flak tower looms ahead! It's too late to give it a wide berth—so you fly right at it. If they're busy keeping their heads down, they won't be busy shooting at you. You open fire. The cupola is enveloped in impact flashes and dust. You sweep past so close you can see chunks of cement crumbling off its sides.

But you can't take care of the tower to your right, and it sends out fingers of antiaircraft fire. This time you hear and feel the flak simultaneously. Your Thunderbolt shudders and yaws drunkenly; it's been struck by a volley of forty-millimeter cannon. Your heart creeps toward your throat.

From your position in the cockpit, you can't see that three cylinder heads have been blown away. But what you feel is plenty disconcerting: the engine, which was running smoothly, is vibrating—badly. It's out of balance. The controls are not as responsive; the fighter wants to roll right. You can see two very large holes in the right wing, and an aileron that does not seem to be doing much when you swing the stick from side to side.

Your plane is severely damaged. You are over enemy-held territory. There is only one thing for it. You struggle to climb higher, stabilize the bird at a speed near 180 MPH . . . collect your wits.

Your radio is quiet. Another aircraft approaches from your right. For a split second you think it's another FW 190. But you're lucky this time, anyway; it's another Thunderbolt. It pulls alongside and looks you over. You can see the pilot's look of disbelief.

The oil tank forward of the cockpit normally holds twenty-eight gallons. It is holed and leaking onto the exhaust/turbocharger return trunking. Though you're not burning, you are leaving a trail of blue-black smoke. The lower third of your cowling is torn away; pieces of it dangle in the slipstream.

At Argentan, still following the rail line, your group turns northwest. You sweep by Falaise and swing due northward, leaving the rail line, still climbing. Caen passes to your left; it's a hornet's nest of antiaircraft fire.

1020 HRS: The antiaircraft fire between Caen and Le Harve is desultory. You pick your way through the cloud deck and cross the coast at about 8,000 feet. Gaps in the white clouds reveal the dark blue-gray of the English Chan-

Ninth Air Force engineers were still constructing many of the forward airfields used by Thunderbolts after D-Day.

nel. Now that you're in a damaged plane, the channel looks far colder and more forbidding than it did on your way in. You're relieved to be

"We were at Nancy, France, and the first commander of the 358th, Colonel Wells, was leading a mission.

"I had the red flight. We flew just across the river at Nancy, along the east side. The Germans were massing their troops, and we flew right over them. Wells came back around and flew right over them again. I just pulled my flight out to the side to avoid the concentrated fire.

"Well, they got him — and when he bailed out, he didn't dive at his wing. He must have just jumped. The tail section took off the top of his head. Our own ground troops found him later, dead."

— Billie Snell, Ninth Air Force, 358th Fighter Group, 367th Squadron

flying at all.

1058 HRS: Landfall! You hang back as the other aircraft of your squadron orbit and touch down. Only then do you throttle back slightly and begin your descent. One other P-47 has stayed with you and will shepherd you in.

1105 HRS: The field is in sight. It seems as though the entire base has turned out for the return. There are crew chiefs and their assistants, armorers, radio men, fuel and oil men, flight chiefs from each section, flight surgeons, firemen, medics. The many who made this mission possible are waiting and watching.

You recheck the gun-arming switch on your left and flip the gun-safety switch just behind it up, to OFF.

You slow down and approach the pattern speed of 150 MPH. When you attempt to crank open the canopy, it hangs up on some jagged metal. You force it.

You set the mixture control to AUTO-RICH and the supercharger, which hasn't really been used since takeoff, to OFF. The propeller you adjust to 2,350 rpm.

Once your speed has dropped below 195 MPH, your left hand rolls the flap control aft.

Simultaneously, you apply forward pressure on the stick to maintain level flight . . . and the nose drops through the horizon!

Damn! No flaps?!

A quick glance at the hydraulic pressure gauge confirms what you suspect:

No hydraulic pressure!

Your stomach knots. Hydraulic pressure runs the flaps.

Your training kicks in. Without hydraulic pressure, you have no flaps, gear, or brakes. But there is a manual pump . . . You can pump down flaps manually . . .

You move the handle next to your left knee up and down a few times, but the needle on the gauge stays put. Nothing . . .

You swing the landing gear lever down. There will be no satisfying double-clunk as the gears drop and lock. You have to yaw the plane from side to side . . . You hear a clunk!

As you throttle back farther the engine runs rougher and rougher. The plane is shaking so much that reading the airspeed indicator is almost impossible. "Engine off" approach speed is around 125 MPH. You are back to "listening to your airspeed," just as you did when you flew the Kaydet biplane in basic.

1108 HRS: The Pratt & Whitney seizes on final approach. Instinctively, you push the stick forward to keep your airspeed from bleeding away. The left main gear splinters a perimeter treetop. The P-47 slews left, and the ground rushes upward.

Six tons of fighter slam into the ground, leaving a huge gash. The right main gear folds up. Now the Jug slews to the right. The horizon tips crazily. Dirt, grass, and small scraps of metal scatter in its wake.

Everything goes quiet. There is no engine sound. Your hands are still gripping the stick. Your eyes snap open. A cloud of dust and fumes swirls away in the breeze, its motion made eerie by the utter silence.

Such a complete silence—at once both unsettling and soothing.

Then you smell them: gas fumes! You hear shouting as the fire crews begin to converge.

Your dazed brain conjures the image of an inferno, spurring your body to action.

A swipe of your left hand opens the quick-release harness. You bolt upward, out of the seat. When you're almost clear, your head snaps backward. You lean back into the cockpit, pull the radio headset plug, spin around, and slide over the wing root's leading edge. You set off in a stumbling run to get clear.

The fire brigade douses your smoldering P-47.

You try to shrug off the medical crew, but the flight surgeon grounds you for the rest of the day. Your crew chief feigns annoyance and horror at how you have returned "his plane."

You dump your parachute and Mae West and flop down in the back of the first vehicle that can take you to interrogation.

Already, the gasoline and oil trucks have begun making their rounds. Camera specialists are removing and replacing the trigger-activated gun cameras in the wing roots. Armorers examine the guns and change the odd worn-looking barrel. Mechanics uncover engines to look for damage and oil leaks, check the tires, and pursue countless other details of routine maintenance. New drop tanks are fitted and filled; fresh ammunition is loaded onto planes that need it. Radio men check the transmitters and receivers.

The engineering section looks over your plane. The engine is scrap; most of the cowling has been blown away. The right wing, bent and riddled with holes, will need to be replaced. The right gear strut has pulled nearly free from its mount. The work of small arms shows in the countless holes in the fuselage and wings. Miraculously, the flak that made the bigger holes aft of the cockpit seems not to have hit anything vital. The radio mast is gone, and the antenna wire is a tangled heap behind the rudder. The engineers shake their heads. Either the third echelon maintenance group will get your Thunderbolt, or she will be cannibalized for parts by fourth echelon.

Resigned to the loss of one bird, the squadron engineering sections then consult with the

USAAF ground crews worked on their airplanes in every type of weather.

flight chiefs to determine which planes are due for routine inspection, which require minor overnight repairs, and which will take longer to fix. Squadron operations passes this information along to group operations. Group sends this information further upstairs, where it will be determined how many aircraft are available for tomorrow's mission.

At debriefing, you are queried about every facet of your flight: Was the weather as predicted? Did the German fighters attack from one direction, more than one direction? How about flak over the target and elsewhere? Did you see any kind of group movement, whether of troops or tanks?

Finally, you and your squadron mates scurry off to chow—and another briefing.

1245 HRS: Another engine start: Forty-four freshly fueled and armed Thunderbolts trundle along the taxiways, off on the day's second mission.

You watch your squadron mates depart. For now, you're glad to be on the ground. You are also certain that no other fighter in the Army Air Force could have sustained such damage and still brought you home.

Two hours later every last one of your brothers-in-arms returns.

1830 HRS: The shadows lengthen as the last Thunderbolts return from the day's third mission. You want to thank personally the pilot who stayed with you this morning, but he is not among the returnees. Later you will learn that he was picked up by Air Sea Rescue.

You get to describe your harrowing flight again and again. Parts of the mission unreel in your mind in slow motion.

You turn in. Tonight you are lucky: sleep comes quickly.

• • •

The P-47's effectiveness was not limited to ground pounding; it was also applauded for its role in armored column cover missions. Perfected by IXth TAC, a close partnership be-

Returning from a mission, Thunderbolts break for landing.

In this typical scene, on a USAAF base in England, Thunderbolt pilots are gathered around a stove in a squadron Nissen hut. USAFM

tween air and armored forces was developed in Normandy and persisted as the Allies pushed into Germany.

In Italy, the British had started using "contact cars," mobile control posts traveling with armored forces that enabled tactical air units to know the precise locations of friendly and enemy forces at all times. Brig. Gen. Elwood Quesada, commander of IXth TAC, developed a similar system for U.S. forces in Normandy. An M4 Sherman tank carried an air liaison officer and a tank commander from the armored forces; AAF personnel made up the rest of the crew. The tank commander communicated with his fellow tankers via an SCR-528 radio;

the air liaison officer used an SCR-522 to coordinate with the column cover flight. Column cover flights consisted of four P-47s that were relieved every thirty minutes.

As an aerial weapons platform, the Thunderbolt was extremely effective at eliminating enemy forces in the path of the Allied advance. Not even heavily armored German tanks were immune to its eight .50-caliber machine guns. After addressing immediate support needs, a fighter flight leader would patrol as far as thirty miles ahead of the armored column, along its axis of advance. Such intensive searches for enemy vehicles, troops, and artillery were often fruitful. Thunderbolts and their British coun-

terparts, Hawker Typhoons, became the aerial eyes and fists of their respective armies.

Meanwhile, experimentation with the P-47's basic design hadn't ended with the ubiquitous D model. Proposed in November 1942 to push the envelope of the original design, the light J model was the fastest version of the Thunderbolt ever built. Rather than a conversion of an existing P-47's structure, XP-47J's was a completely new airframe. Republic engineers lightened the wing and reduced the armament to six .50-caliber machine guns. The engine was a 2,800-horsepower Pratt & Whitney R-2800-57(C) housed inside a close-fitting cowling and cooled by a fan. Engineers separated the ventral intake for the CH-5 turbosupercharger from the engine cowling and moved it aft. They also fitted a conical-shaped spinner to the four-bladed propeller. The XP-47J flew for the first time on November 26, 1943; on August 4, 1944, it became the first propeller-driven fighter to exceed 500 MPH, achieving 507 MPH at 34,300 feet.

The P-47M was another version of the Thunderbolt designed with an eye toward achieving top speed. It didn't carry underwing racks for external stores. The P-47M's mission was to destroy German V-1 "Buzz Bombs." To that end, it was also fitted with the Pratt & Whitney R-2800-57(C) engine, equipped with a CH-5 turbosupercharger. The engine offered a war emergency power of 2,800 horsepower at 32,500 feet with water injection. Fewer than 140 of the M variant were made, and engine difficulties kept them largely out of the fray until the closing weeks of the war. The M's maximum speeds included 400 MPH at 10,000 feet; 453 MPH at 25,000 feet; and 470 MPH at 30,000 feet.

The P-47N, designed specifically for the Pacific Theater of Operations (PTO), was the last production version of the Thunderbolt. As an escort for B-29 Superfortresses flying all the way from Saipan to Japan, it gave excellent service in the PTO during 1945. The P-47N's success was due in large part to its remarkable similarities to a flying gas can. Eight additional

The XP-47J was the first propeller-driven fighter to exceed 500 MPH. USAFM

tanks—one on the leading edge of each wing and three near each landing gear well—swelled its fuel capacity to an impressive 1,266 gallons. That capacity made possible a maximum range of 2,350 miles.

The P-47N's landing gear was, by necessity, stronger and of slightly wider track than the gear of earlier variants. In addition to the eight .50-caliber machine guns, it could carry two 500-pound bombs and ten five-inch rockets. The maximum weight of the P-47N was over 20,000 pounds! Wing surface area was increased by twenty-two square feet and featured larger ailerons and squared-off wingtips. These innovations enhanced the roll rate and maneuverability of the P-47N. The dorsal fin, behind the bubble canopy, was somewhat larger than that of the P-47D, a modification that improved directional stability.

A total of 1,667 P-47Ns were produced by the Farmingdale plant between December 1944 and December 1945. At the Evansville factory, 149 P-47Ns were built. V-J Day brought the cancellation of nearly 6,000 Thunderbolts. Production ceased shortly thereafter. The last P-47N was rolled out in September 1945, thus ending the largest production run of any American fighter. A total of 15,683 Thunderbolts had been built.

P-47D and N Thunderbolts remained in use by the United States Air Force (USAF) for several years after the war, serving with TAC, Strategic Air Command, and Air Defense Command squadrons. The models' redesignation as F-47D and F-47N coincided with the 1948 creation of the USAF. They eventually reached Air National Guard squadrons. The last American Thunderbolts were phased out of service in 1955.

Despite their reassignment to the lower regions toward the end of 1944, Thunderbolts racked up an impressive number of air-to-air kills throughout the remainder of the war. Thunderbolt veterans may take particular pleasure in pointing out that by war's end P-47s had destroyed more Luftwaffe aircraft

than the vaunted P-51 Mustang had.

The Fifty-sixth FG was particularly successful; it destroyed 1,006 German aircraft against a loss of 128 Thunderbolts—a ratio of nearly eight to one. Those figures made the Fifty-sixth the top aerial scoring group in the Army Air Force. Its pilots had faith in their mounts and a superb commander in the person of Col. Hubert "Hub" Zemke. They operated Thunderbolts through to the end of the war in Europe.

And it wasn't just the German air force that suffered; P-47 bombing and strafing campaigns beat up the Wehrmacht on the ground.

Given the Thunderbolt's numbers and versatility, its phaseout seems incongruously rapid. In the run-up to Overlord, IXth TAC fielded no fewer than eleven fighter groups flying nearly eight hundred of these aircraft. By 1947, only three or four groups in the Occupation Forces were equipped with P-47s. The rest of the Thunderbolt armada had been gathered up and destroyed in a postwar demobilization frenzy. None were deployed in Korea five years later.

There is little question that the Thunderbolt distinguished itself as a potent tactical air weapon in western Europe, that it was reliable and easy to fly. It was also tenacious, and the P-47's highest praise has always come from the men who flew her. She brought them back.

"There was an air force pilot in a tank up in the front lines. When they needed our help, they'd call us and give us the grid coordinates.

"A big puff of red smoke comes up.

" 'Strafe that area, those woods, about one hundred yards north of the red smoke.'

"We went up there, and we worked it up and down.

"The controller called back and said, 'You did all right. Thanks, fellas. So long!'

"We never knew what was there. . . or even whether there was anything there."

— Charles W. Cassidy, Ninth Air Force, 358th Fighter Group, 367th Squadron

Gen. "Pete" Quesada (right) helped USAFM
establish tactical support and close cooperation between the air forces and infantry.

Previous pages: The P-47 shown here is a block D model; its bubble canopy vastly increased visibility—and survivability—during the fighter pilot's mission. The wide stance and massive radial engine, which suggest sturdiness and reliability, were also features of earlier models. The tapered fuselage earned the "Jug" its nickname. This restored fighter's markings are those of Col. David Schilling, commander of the Fifty-sixth Fighter Group.

The control surfaces of early model P-47s were covered with fabric. While fabric-covered surfaces are lighter and therefore easier for the pilot to maneuver during combat, the big Republic fighter, nearly unmatched in a dive, generated such force when it shot earthward that it tended to shed the fabric on its rear surfaces. This Thunderbolt's elevators and rudder are metal covered.

Under the canopy rail are Colonel Schilling's aerial victory markings; each cross represents a downed German aircraft. Schilling ended the war with twenty-three victories.

This page: The wide track of the P-47's undercarriage allowed the fighter to use forward airfields with hastily prepared runways, often dirt that only recently had been the front line. Two of the fighter's trademarks are visible here: at left, the huge twelve-foot propeller that fronts the radial engine; at right, three of the eight .50-caliber machine guns that made this airplane such a deadly ground-attack weapon.

USAFM

A

A   In contrast to the fighter shown in the previous four photos, this Thunderbolt is an earlier model and carries the "razorback" fuselage aft of the cockpit. In aerial combat, a fighter pilot's survival depended upon his ability to see the enemy before the enemy saw him; the streamlined fuselage shown here created an often deadly blind spot.

B   The pilot's view as he climbed onto the wing and approached the cockpit. The heavily glazed canopy, rolled back here, also contributed to the poor visibility in early Thunderbolts. Behind the pilot's seat is an armored plate 1/4" thick; at the top, the pilot's headrest is covered with well-worn brown leather.

"Dutch" Biel Collection

B

C When the P-47 arrived in the ETO, fighter command worried that the hefty Republic fighter would be confused with the German FW 190, which was also powered by a radial engine, in the heat of combat. So that pilots would know by sight who was friend and who was foe, USAAF fighters were decked with white cowlings and white stripes on their wings. The risk of confusion was further diminished by the fact that, when viewed head on, the Thunderbolt has an oval shape that's quite distinctive. The engine cowling narrows into an elegant curve that houses the turbosupercharger ductwork, which runs along the bottom of the fuselage. It's this ductwork and machinery that makes the Thunderbolt look like a single-engine fighter, and an oversized one at that. Compared to the Spitfire, the P-47 was huge. Legend has it that when some RAF personnel saw the American fighter for the first time, they waited around to see the rest of the crew get out long after the pilot had walked away.

C

B

A   To accommodate the space needed for the four-gun weapons bay in the wing and provide ground clearance for the propeller, a special undercarriage was designed for the P-47. Most unorthodox was the landing gear, which telescoped and was nine inches shorter when retracted than when extended. To the surprise of some observers, the innovation caused few problems in the field.

B   High-performance fighters needed sizable flaps in order to land at a reasonable speed on some of the shorter runways in use during WWII. The flaps were also critical tools in combat; pilots could use small degrees of flap extension to tighten a turn and bring their guns to bear on the enemy.

C   The strut of the P-47's rugged main wheel. The split doors on the outside of the strut move back and forth as the gear extends and contracts during flight operations.

C

DWG. NO. G507A-0
SER. NO. P275473
ANGLE LOW 23.0
ANGLE HIGH 56.0

DWG. NO. G507A-0
SER. NO. P275472
ANGLE LOW 23.0
ANGLE HIGH 56.0

DWG. NO. G507A-0
SER. NO. P275474
ANGLE LOW 23.0
ANGLE HIGH 56.0

DWG. NO. G507A-0
SER. NO. P275475
ANGLE LOW 23.0
ANGLE HIGH 56.0

A

A   The heart of the beast is the Pratt & Whitney R-2800; the air-cooled power plant is one of the most reliable aircraft engines ever constructed. Thunderbolts sometimes returned to base with several cylinders shot away and the engine still running. One-bullet damage to the radiator of a P-51 Mustang, by contrast, left the pilot about nine minutes before the coolant-starved engine overheated and seized.

   After the Mustang assumed bomber escort duties, P-47 Thunderbolts of the Eighth and Ninth Air Forces proved to be outstanding ground-attack fighter-bombers. One reason for their success was the ability of the R-2800 to withstand withering ground fire.

   Beneath the circular engine is the duct entry for the turbosupercharger system.

B   The R-2800, seen here on an engine stand, didn't power only the P-47 Thunderbolt; it also took the Martin B-26 Marauder, Grumman F6F Hellcat, Chance-Vought F4U Corsair, and the Curtiss C-46 Commando to war and

back. Ground crews often worked through the night in inclement conditions to keep these stalwart engines in working order. Sometimes this entailed changing cylinders, called "jugs," that were damaged by enemy fire or the stress of running in the war emergency power setting.

USAFM

B

Previous page: The P-47 carried eight .50-caliber machine guns, which amounted to a devastating degree of firepower at the point where all the rounds converged. Lethal for aircraft, this weight of fire proved equally deadly when turned upon such ground targets as trucks, locomotives, tanks, and troops. The ground crew's armorers were responsible for refilling the gun bays with the long belts of .50-caliber cartridges. This Thunderbolt required several wooden cases' worth of the heavy ammunition.

A The tools of an armorer in the Army Air Force. Beneath the wing and inboard of the left main wheel sit cases of .50-caliber ammunition. Ammunition belts were assembled elsewhere on the air base. The tip of every fifth shell was painted red to tag it a tracer, a phosphorous-containing bullet that ignited when fired and enabled the pilot to track his aim. In the foreground is the armorer's chest, which carries the tools essential to maintaining the machine guns. On top of the box is a thermos of GI coffee and a lightweight jacket; inside it is a symbol of home—a well-worn baseball glove.

B Red tape applied to the guns after the armorers had completed their work marked a fighter as armed and mission ready.

C A small movie camera ran whenever the guns were fired; here it's being loaded into a bay just under the leading edge of the right wing.

A

A   Pilots generally felt that the cockpit of the P-47 Thunderbolt was roomy and comfortable, especially when compared to that of the Supermarine Spitfire or the Messerschmitt Bf 109. Under the gunsight, on the left side of the panel, are the artificial horizon, gyrocompass, turn-and-bank indicator, altimeter, and airspeed indicator. To the right of the yellow line are the engine instruments, the pilot's window on the health of his power plant.

B   American fighters were fitted with a pistol grip at the top of the control stick. The firing button for the guns is on the front of the grip.

C   The Thunderbolt's engine controls are at the pilot's left. The large silver handle that dominates the array is the throttle. The fuel-air mixture is controlled by the dark red knob, and a

B

turn of the black knob marked P adjusts the pitch of the propeller. During the long climb and cruise of escort missions, the pilot used these controls to conserve his fuel, maintaining his ability to engage in aerial combat and still get back to base. When the fighter operated from forward bases in a ground support role, the enemy was often only minutes away, making careful fuel management less imperative.

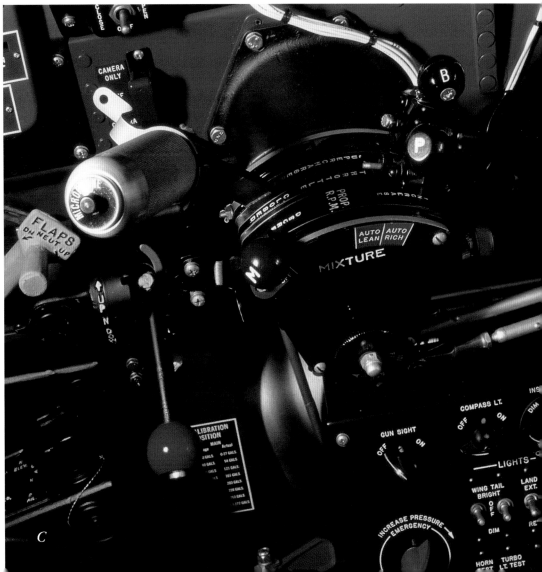

C

A   Directly in front of the pilot is the K-14 computing gunsight. This sight projected a ring of lights on the angled glass through which the pilot looked as he flew in combat. An enemy fighter brought inside the ring of lights came under the converging fire of the P-47's eight .50-caliber machine guns.

B   The graduated scale above the sight is marked with the types of aircraft the fighter pilot might encounter.

C   The tail antennae shown here were part of the warning radar system, which alerted the pilot to unidentified aircraft approaching from his rear or the six o'clock position.

D   The red light glowed when the tail warning system detected an unknown aircraft.

E   Handles just above the stick released bombs or drop tanks carried under the wings.

USAFM

42

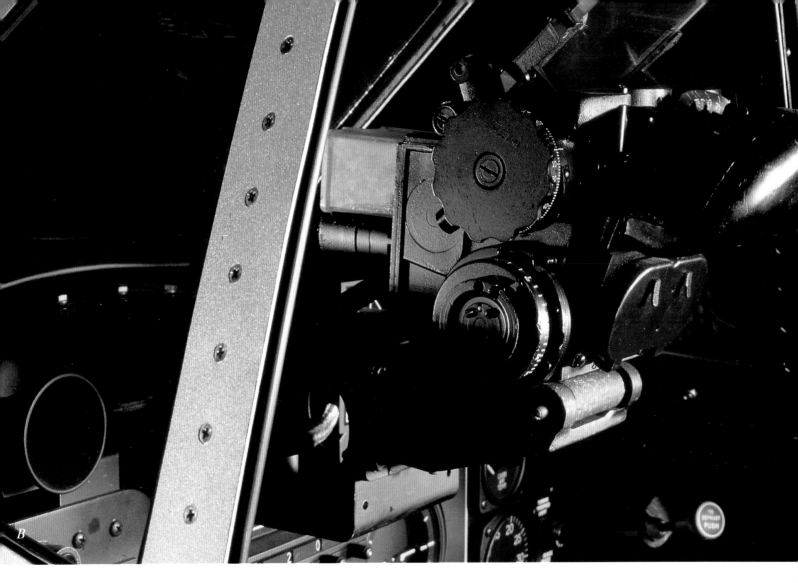

B

C

E

BOMB OR TANK RELEASE

PARK

LANDING GEAR WARNING LIGHTS

12 8 DAYS

3

6

9

DIRECTIONAL GYRO

D

B

A   The bubble canopy provided the fighter pilot with excellent visibility.

B   In part because a spot or smudge on the windscreen could hide an attacking fighter from the pilot's view, aircraft ground crews looked after "their" airplanes very carefully.

C   The headrest was supported by a steel plate that protected the pilot in the event of an attack from the rear.

C

A

A   Pilots and fighters weren't the only ones tested by aerial combat. The enlisted men of the maintenance crews worked at all hours to keep these warbirds effective and in the air.

B

B   A typical ground crew consisted of two and sometimes three enlisted men. At the least, a crew chief was responsible for the well-being of the fighter, and an armorer maintained the weapons systems. At air bases in England, specialists maintained radios and avionics; they also handled major engine repair and minor airframe repair. Severely damaged fighters were either taken to a repair depot for major work or written off and replaced. The constant stream of new fighters supplied by America's wartime industry far outstripped loss of airplanes.

C   Ground crews were scrupulous about keeping the scoreboards on the sides of their fighters up-to-date.

C

A

B

48

A   Prior to a sortie, the pilot performs a walk-around inspection of his craft. The crew chief walks with him, reviewing the mission's fuel and weapons requirements. While ground crews are responsible for the systems and the airframe, a single-seat fighter pilot must assure himself that his P-47 will perform as expected. His life depends upon it.

B   The pilot checks the air intake for obstructions.

C   A pilot can detect loose panels, leaking fluids, and other problems by running his hand over the skin of the fighter. Late in the war, the USAAF issued pilots green fabric flight jackets with alpaca collars. These replaced the symbol of the American fighter pilot: the leather A-2 jacket.

C

226641

TAB ADJUSTED AT FACTORY
DO NOT TOUCH

A

A   Before takeoff, pilots preview their mission with maps of the target and en route checkpoints. The pilot at left is wearing an RAF life vest and flight helmet; some American pilots preferred RAF equipment and used it throughout the war.

B

A   Standing behind the wing of his fighter, this pilot wears a combination of standard-issue American flight gear and RAF equipment. Over his green B-10 jacket he wears a USAAF-issue life vest; the "Mae West," as it was called, was required for over-water flights. He also wears an RAF flight helmet and goggles with an American oxygen mask attached.

B   Fighter pilots wore a heavy and cumbersome seat-style parachute that was often strapped on just before they entered the cockpit. For flights over water, this pack also included an inflatable dinghy and other essentials.

C   Once over the cockpit rail, the pilot grabs the top of the windscreen to lower himself into his fighter.

C

A

A   As Mustangs took over as bomber escorts, Thunderbolts were pressed into successful service as close-support, ground-attack fighter-bombers. This Thunderbolt is in the markings of the 513th Fighter Squadron, Ninth Air Force, which provided air cover for the advancing infantry. The Ninth's General Quesada put pilots and USAAF radio equipment in the tanks of General Patton's Third Army, thereby inventing interservice tactical cooperation. This view of a low-flying Thunderbolt is how countless infantrymen remember the "Jug."

Next pages: The Thunderbolt in its element.

Acknowledgments

The B-10 jacket pictured on page 4 was supplied by Eastman Leather Clothing. Interested parties can contact Eastman by telephone at 44 1752 896874; by fax at 44 1752 690579; or by E-mail at eastman@eastmanleather.demon.co.uk.

The photographs in this book would not have been possible without the considerable help of the following individuals and organizations:

Butch Schroeder, Midwest Aviation Museum, Danville, Illinois. Butch owns and operates the finest flying restorations of World War II fighters. His attention to detail and historical accuracy was invaluable to this project. The Thunderbolt showcased here is just one example of his commitment to excellence; he also flies *Little Margaret*, the warbird that was the primary subject for *Mustang: North American P-51*, another book in this series.

Mike Vad bon Couer, Midwest Aero Restorations Ltd., Danville, Illinois. Mike is the talented airframe and power plant expert who resurrected the fighters that Butch Schroeder owns and flies. Always ready to help and answer questions, Mike is one of the reasons that these books look the way they do. I cannot thank him enough.

Charles Osborn and Brad Hood, Vintage Fighters, Jeffersonville, Indiana. Brad and Charles allowed me my first look at a restored P-47.

The United States Air Force Museum, Gen. Charles Metcalf, USAF (Ret.), Director, Dayton, Ohio. This unique resource, so close to home, is priceless. The "razorback" version of the P-47 is part of its collection, and the Research Center is a treasury of photographs and documents. The center's director is Wes Henry, and Dave Menard maintains the files and knows where everything is. Thanks also to Diana Bachert, Bob Bobbit, Denise Bollinger, Bob Spaulding, and Meryl Morris.

The late Jeff Ethell. Jeff's enthusiasm and friendship pointed me in the right direction.

Bart Reams, Crossroad Coins and Surplus, Dayton, Ohio. Bart is always ready to help and often has that one hard-to-find artifact that makes the books so much better.

Kurt Weidner, Tim Thompson, and Ted Filer. The "crew" made more than a few trips to Illinois to make the photographs that give this book its life. The concept remains the same: these airplanes didn't go anywhere without pilots and ground crew.

Bob Hower. This longtime friend brought his piece of history, a 1948 Hudson Hornet, to Danville for one of the photo sessions. I am indebted to Bob for years of friendship and the great portrait he shot of me for this book. Photographers rarely get their picture taken; we are always behind the camera.

My kids, Nate, Brigitta, and Joe. And my parents, Bill and Jane Patterson, for helping me with the kids when I am chasing airplanes as well as for their ongoing support.

Cheryl Terrill, for her understanding friendship.

Ross and Elinor Howell, Howell Press, Charlottesville, Virginia. Ross continues to believe in and support what I do and how I do it.

Ron Dick, my compatriot, friend, and partner. We keep finding things to do books about.

Paul Perkins, my oldest and closest friend. Since 1965 we have been chasing airplanes and imagining ourselves in the cockpit…Look what happens when you dream.

Technical Notes

The original photography in this book was undertaken with the intention of removing, as faithfully as possible, the clues of the present day and opening, with the help of the owners and operators of these aircraft, a window on the years when formations of these airplanes flew over Europe.

I used a variety of cameras and equipment to complete this project: a Wista 4 x 5 Field View camera with a 150 mm Caltar II lens and a 90 mm Nikkor lens; a Mamiya RB67 with 50 mm, 90 mm, and 180 mm lenses; a Nikon F3 with a motor drive; and a Nikon 8008 with garden-variety Nikkor lenses.

All of the photographs were shot as transparencies, which result in the best possible color separations.

The 4 x 5 and 6 x 7 photos were all shot on Kodak Ektachrome Daylight film. The 35 mm photos were also taken with Ektachrome.

The concept, design, and photographs are those of Dan Patterson, 6825 Peters Pike, Dayton, OH 45414.

For more information about the books of Dan Patterson, Paul Perkins, and Ron Dick, please visit http://www.flyinghistory.com.

Bibliography

AAF: Official World War II Guide to the Army Air Forces. New York: Bonanza Books, 1988.

Angelucci, Enzo, and Peter Bowers. *The American Fighter: The Definitive Guide to American Fighter Aircraft from 1917 to the Present.* New York: Orion Books, 1987.

Bodie, Warren. *Republic's P-47 Thunderbolt: From Seversky to Victory.* Hiawassee, Ga.: Widewing Publications, 1994.

Duxford Diary. Cambridge, England: W. Heffner & Sons, 1945.

Farley, Edward J. *U.S. Army Air Force Fighter Planes P-1 to F-107.* Los Angeles: Aero Publishers, 1961.

Freeman, Roger. *The Mighty Eighth in Color.* Stillwater, Minn.: Specialty Press, 1992.

Freeman, Roger. *The Ninth Air Force in Colour.* London: Arms and Armour Press, 1995.

Freeman, Roger. *Thunderbolt: A Documentary History of the Republic P-47.* London: Macdonald and Jane's Publishers, 1978.

Green, William. *War Planes of the Second World War.* Vol. 4, *Fighters.* New York: Doubleday, 1964.

Hallion, Richard P. *The U.S. Army Air Forces in World War II, D-Day 1944: Air Power over the Normandy Beaches and Beyond.* Online publication available at http://aeroweb.brooklyn.cuny.edu/history/wwii/d-day/toc.html.

Hess, William N. *P-47 Thunderbolt: Warbird History.* Osceola, Wisc.: Motorbooks International, 1994.

Hess, William N. *Zemke's Wolfpack: The 56th Fighter Group in World War II.* Osceola, Wisc.: Motorbooks International, 1992.

Jane's Fighting Aircraft of World War II. New York: Military Press, 1989.

Pilot's Manual for P-47 Thunderbolt. Appleton, Wisc.: Aviation Publications, 1988.

Shacklady, Edward. *The Republic P-47D Thunderbolt: Aircraft in Profile.* New York: Doubleday, 1969.

Swanborough, Gordon, and Peter M. Bowers. *United States Military Aircraft since 1909.* Washington, D.C.: Smithsonian Institution Press, 1989.

Wagner, Ray. *American Combat Planes.* Third ed. New York: Doubleday, 1982.

Bob Hower

Dan Patterson is a self-employed photographer, graphic designer, and private pilot living in Dayton, Ohio. His previous books include *Shoo Shoo Baby: A Lucky Lady of the Sky; The Lady: Boeing B-17 Flying Fortress; The Soldier: Consolidated B-24 Liberator; Mustang: North American P-51; Lancaster: RAF Heavy Bomber; Messerschmitt Bf 109: Luftwaffe Fighter; Spitfire: RAF Fighter; American Eagles: A History of the United States Air Force;* and *Cockpit: An Illustrated History of World War II Aircraft Interiors.*

Paul Perkins is an emergency room physician living in Bloomington, Indiana. He has authored *The Lady: Boeing B-17 Flying Fortress; The Soldier: Consolidated B-24 Liberator;* and *Mustang: North American P-51.*